Enjoy Playing Guitar

Going Solo

25 progressive pieces for the early grades

Debbie Cracknell

MUSIC DEPARTMENT

OXFORD

UNIVERSITY PRESS

OXFORD
UNIVERSITY PRESS

Great Clarendon Street, Oxford OX2 6DP, England

Oxford University Press is a department of the University of Oxford.
It furthers the University's aim of excellence in research, scholarship,
and education by publishing worldwide in

Oxford New York
Auckland Cape Town Hong Kong Karachi
Kuala Lumpur Madrid Melbourne Mexico City Nairobi
New Delhi Shanghai Taipei Toronto

With offices in

Argentina Austria Brazil Chile Czech Republic France Greece
Guatemala Hungary Italy Japan Poland Portugal Singapore
South Korea Switzerland Thailand Turkey Ukraine Vietnam

11

ISBN 978-0-19-338635-8

Music and text origination by
Katie Johnston
Printed in Great Britain on acid-free paper by
Halstan & Co. Ltd, Amersham, Bucks.

All pieces are original compositions by the author unless otherwise stated.
All adaptations are by the author.

CONTENTS

Olé José

Give this piece a lively Spanish feel (**Allegretto** means 'fairly fast and lively'). Strum where indicated (↑↓) in the direction of the arrows, being very careful to hit only the first three strings.

Musette

A musette is a type of French bagpipe which was popular in the seventeenth and eighteenth centuries. Bagpipes make a 'drone'—a continuous note heard throughout the piece—which is imitated here by the bass A. Use a rest stroke for the beginning and ending sections, and free strokes in the middle (bars 9–16). *Pont.* (or *ponticello*) means play near the bridge; *nat.* is back to the natural sound.

Joshua fought the battle of Jericho

Play this well-known spiritual at a lively pace. When you see 'jazz 8ths' or 'swing rhythm' (♫ = ♪♪) at the beginning of a piece, play all the ♫ rhythms long–short. Take care with the fingering at bar 10 to produce an Am chord. The final chord is all taken at the fifth fret on the first three strings. An alternative fingering would be to use a half barré.

Allegretto

African-American Spiritual

Sussex Carol

Like 'Musette', this piece uses a drone bass. It could be accompanied by a small drum, which would add a traditional early English flavour; the rhythm ♩. ♩ ♪ will work for most of the piece, but bars 16 and 17 would need the simpler rhythm of ♩. ♩. ♩. | ♩. ♩. to fit in with the change of time signature.

Trad. (English)

Ländler

A Ländler is a folk dance which originated in Austria and parts of Germany. Always in three time, it is often said to be the forerunner of the waltz. The D chord shape (as used in bar 1) occurs in six bars in this piece so practise it separately first. Use a free stroke throughout. **Moderato** means 'at a moderate pace'.

Joseph Küffner
(1776–1856)

Lullaby

Give this a gentle feel (**Tranquillo** means 'calm and gentle'). Bring out the melody line where indicated by the accents (>). Take care to hold all the dotted minims (♩.) and tied notes for their full value. The ❜ is a 'comma pause'—take a slight break before the next phrase. The *gliss.* (or *glissando*) is a slide, so at the end of this piece, slide the fourth finger from the G to the B.

Pepé's Sombrero

This is a typical Spanish-sounding piece, using running passages in the bass (bars 1–8 and 25–32) and repeated top notes (bars 17–24), as found in much flamenco music. Keep the two-note chords in the first and last sections quieter than the tune in the bass.

Ding dong! merrily on high

This is an old French tune which is still popular today as a Christmas carol. **Vivace** means 'lively', so aim for a feeling of two in a bar. Be careful to alternate *i* and *m* fingers of the right hand throughout the piece; the thumb, of course, keeps to the bass-line. Note that this piece is all played in the second position.

16th-century French

The Celtic Cross

Written in the style of Celtic folk music, this piece needs to move along at a good pace (**Allegro** means 'fast and lively'). Be sure to make the contrasts of volume and timbre (different tones, e.g. *ponticello*) on the repeats. Strum the A chord on the last line in the direction of the arrows. Finish with the last chord played tambora—hit the strings very near the bridge with the right-hand thumb.

Robin's Revel

This piece is in the style of the lute music common in Elizabethan times. Aim for a speed of ♩. = 68; a feeling of one dotted minim (♩.) in a bar will help the music move along. Keep the dotted rhythms very crisp, and use *ponticello* where shown to give this piece its early-music feel.

Coconut Corn

Use the expression signs (particularly the accents) to keep this piece in a lively Caribbean style. Take care to slide the D chord shape in bar 30 up two frets in bar 31 so the right-hand arpeggio can then be played as normal. End with a short, sharp chord, indicated by the staccato dots above and below the notes.

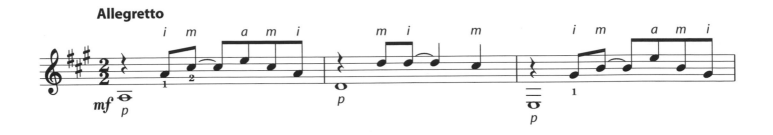

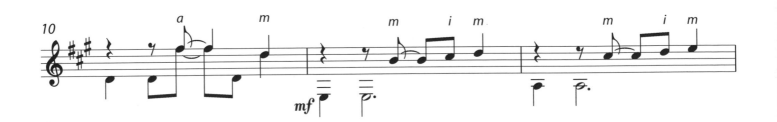

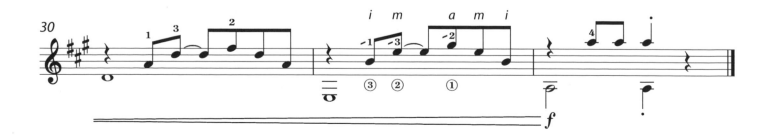

A Strange Dream

Keep the speed steady and give the piece a calm, dream-like quality. Five beats to a bar is an unusual time signature (perhaps this dream was *very* strange). Use the accents in bars 9, 10, 13, and 14 to shift the emphasis on to the first and fourth beats. When you see a pause sign (⌢) on the last note of a piece, pause slightly *before* the note to create the best effect.

Carnival in the Rain

The South American rhythm is lively, but the minor key gives this piece a slightly sad feel. Note the **meno mosso** ('less movement') in the last two bars, and play more slowly. Enjoy the very high A at the end—it's on the 17th fret of the first string!

The Foggy Dew

This is a straightforward English folk tune, but watch the rhythm in bar 14. Care with the left-hand fingering will help to keep the melody line smooth.

The Willow Tree

Phrase marks (long curved lines above a group of bars) help to divide a piece into 'sentences'. Take a 'breath'—a very slight pause—at the end of a phrase, and it will help to give the music shape.

Downtown Doodle

This piece is much easier than it first appears. Don't be put off by all the sharps in the key signature (E major); the piece actually all lies comfortably under the fingers. Play at a steady swing (**Andante** means 'at walking pace') and allow the bass notes to ring on as indicated. *Simile* means 'the same' and refers to these bass notes throughout the piece.

Apache Dance

There are some high positions in this one! However, everything fits the hand well if you keep to the given left-hand fingering and string numbers. When playing the tambora passages, hit only strings 4, 5, and 6 while holding down the Em chord.

Skye Boat Song

Like 'Musette', this Scottish tune has a drone in the first and last sections, to imitate the sound of the Scottish bagpipe. This bass G makes the piece more difficult than it looks, although it stays in first position throughout. Hold the G with the third finger in bars 1–12 and 21–32, and use the fourth finger for all the second-string Ds.

Trad. (Scottish)

Athena's Dance

Written in a Greek style, this piece uses repeated semiquavers (♫), which are common in music for the bouzouki—a long-necked metal-strung instrument, usually played with a plectrum. As usual, use alternate right-hand fingers *i* and *m* on the melody line. Note the change of key from A minor to D minor (B♭ in the key signature) at bar 17. The ⌁ sign indicates a mordent (optional here)—play the main note, then the note above (in the scale), then the main note again (C–D–C in bar 7, F–G–F in bar 23), all very rapidly and all slurred.

On the High Plateau

The diamond-shaped notes are harmonics, produced by touching the string lightly with the left hand exactly above the metal of the fret indicated and plucking normally with the right, which causes a ringing effect. Strings are indicated in circles, and fret numbers as normal figures. The small note in bars 5 and 9 is an *acciaccatura* (a 'crushed' note)—play it on the beat with a fast slur to the main note. Let the tied semibreve (o) Es ring on like a church bell heard in the distance.

Vals Fácil

The waltz (*vals*) was a popular dance in the nineteenth century, especially in Vienna. This one was composed by the Spanish guitarist and composer Daniel Fortea, a pupil of the famous guitar composer Tárrega. The slurs in bars 1 and 5 are best taken on frets 4 and 5, moving across the strings; use the following open bass A to move back into first position. In the second half, try to hold the fingered bass notes for their full value to keep the arpeggios sounding *legato* (smooth).

Daffodil Waltz

This is another waltz (see 'Vals Fácil'); aim for at least ♩. = 50 to keep the dance moving. A little emphasis on the first beat of each bar will keep your imaginary dancers in step. The wavy line next to the final chord indicates that it should be spread.

Nashville Nick

This has the style of American country music and needs to sound laid-back! The piece may look simple on the page, but the F chord at bars 11, 12, 27, and 28 will take practice—you need to flatten your first finger across both the C and the F. Use the right-hand thumb for all the bass notes (the melody), and strum lightly with *i* down/up, across the first three strings on all the chords. *Simile* refers to these chords—carry on strumming down/up throughout the piece. Yee-haa!

Moondust

Lento misterioso means 'slow and mysterious'. This piece is much easier than it looks as it consists mainly of sliding left-hand fingers 2 and 3 together up and down the fingerboard on strings 1 and 2. Slow right down at the end with a *pianissimo* (**pp** = very soft) last chord.

Those Homework Blues!

We all know the feeling! The *acciaccaturas* in bars 1, 3, 5, and 7 are to be played with a slide to the main note; this is indicated by a straight slide line as well as the curved slur line. Remember that *acciaccaturas* are played *on* the beat, i.e. with the bass note, not before it.